# A PET WHAT?!

# MY PET MINI PIG

## BY PAIGE V. POLINSKY

EPIC

BELLWETHER MEDIA • MINNEAPOLIS, MN

Action and adventure collide in EPIC.
Plunge into a universe of powerful
beasts, hair-raising tales, and high-speed
excitement. Astonishing explorations await.
Can you handle it?

This edition first published in 2020 by Bellwether Media, Inc.

No part of this publication may be reproduced in whole or in part without written permission of the publisher.
For information regarding permission, write to Bellwether Media, Inc., Attention: Permissions Department,
6012 Blue Circle Drive, Minnetonka, MN 55343.

Library of Congress Cataloging-in-Publication Data

Names: Polinsky, Paige V., author.
Title: My pet mini pig / Paige V. Polinsky.
Description: Minneapolis, MN : Bellwether Media, 2020. | Series: A pet
    what?! | Includes bibliographical references and index. | Audience: Ages
    7-12. | Audience: Grades 4-6. | Summary: "Engaging images accompany
    information about pet mini pigs. The combination of high-interest
    subject matter and light text is intended for students in grades 2
    through 7"– Provided by publisher.
Identifiers: LCCN 2019034521 (print) | LCCN 2019034522 (ebook) | ISBN
    9781644871843 (library binding) | ISBN 9781618918703 (ebook)
Subjects: LCSH: Miniature pigs as pets–Juvenile literature. | Miniature
    pigs–Juvenile literature. | Swine as pets–Juvenile literature.
Classification: LCC SF393.M55 P65 2020  (print) | LCC SF393.M55  (ebook) |
    DDC 636.4/0887–dc23
LC record available at https://lccn.loc.gov/2019034521
LC ebook record available at https://lccn.loc.gov/2019034522

Editor: Betsy Rathburn       Designer: Josh Brink

Printed in the United States of America, North Mankato, MN.

# TABLE OF CONTENTS

# PLAYFUL AND PINK

A spotted pink mini pig splashes in a puddle.
It digs through the mud with its rubbery **snout**.

snout

Mini pigs are playful little pets. They are also very smart!

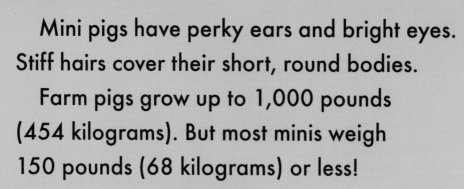

Mini pigs have perky ears and bright eyes. Stiff hairs cover their short, round bodies. Farm pigs grow up to 1,000 pounds (454 kilograms). But most minis weigh 150 pounds (68 kilograms) or less!

## SUPER SNIFFERS

Like all pigs, mini pigs have a powerful sense of smell. A mini's snout is 2,000 times stronger than a human nose!

# MINI PIG PROFILE

- **Animal Type:** mammal
- **Life Span:** up to 20 years
- **Height:** up to 30 inches (76 centimeters)
- **Weight:** up to 150 pounds (68 kilograms)

Many different **breeds** are called mini pigs.
Potbellied pigs are most common.

potbellied pig

Mini pigs do not stay small forever. People
must be sure they can care for a full-grown mini.
**Rescues** can help people **adopt** one!

# PIG PENS

Mini pigs like to be outside. They need fenced pens with fresh water.

These pigs are very friendly. They are happiest with other pigs around. Minis can also get along with dogs and cats!

## MUD ARMOR

Mud protects mini pigs from bug bites. It also keeps them cool on hot days.

# MINI PIG PEN

fence

blankets

shelter

water

food

Mini pigs can learn to use the bathroom outside. Inside, they should have a **litter pan**.

Playpens give minis safe spaces inside. Some minis sleep in playpens at night. Others cuddle with their owners!

# MINI PIG CARE DUTIES

## Daily
- ☑ feed and water
- ☑ play and exercise
- ☑ brush teeth
- ☑ clean litter pan

## Weekly
- ☑ brush hair

## Yearly
- ☑ bring to vet
- ☑ trim hooves and tusks

## As Needed
- ☑ full bath

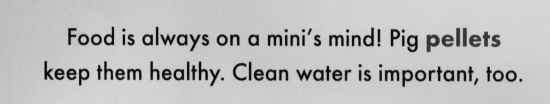

Food is always on a mini's mind! Pig **pellets** keep them healthy. Clean water is important, too.

grazing

## CRUMB HUNTERS

Mini pigs will open doors to search for snacks. Owners must keep food and trash locked up tight!

Minis also love fresh fruits and veggies. They like to **graze** on grass and hay.

# HAPPY AND HEALTHY

Mini pigs can be bossy! They may nip or beg for food. Owners must teach them manners. Owners should also keep track of feeding. **Obesity** is a common problem in minis. Vet visits are important!

## BRAIN FOOD

Mini pigs are fast learners. Owners can reward them with food for a job well done.

# MINI PIG HEALTH SUPPLIES

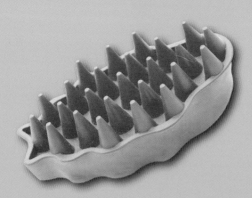

rubber brush

shampoo

toothbrush

leash and harness
for vet visits

Mini pigs only need baths when they are muddy.

But they need other care more often.
Mini pigs need their hair and teeth brushed.
Their hooves and **tusks** should be trimmed
every year.

Minis need places to **root**. They love to go outside. They will also root in blankets.

These happy pets need a lot of care.
They are not easy animals. But they are
wonderful friends!

# GLOSSARY

**adopt**—to take in as a pet

**breeds**—different types of pigs

**graze**—to eat grass or other plants growing in a field

**litter pan**—a pan filled with dry material used as an indoor toilet for animals

**obesity**—the unhealthy state of being overweight

**pellets**—small, hard balls of food

**rescues**—places from which people can adopt animals in need of homes

**root**—to look for food by digging through the ground with the nose

**snout**—the long nose of some animals

**tusks**—long teeth that stick out of the mouth of some animals

# TO LEARN MORE

## AT THE LIBRARY

Polinsky, Paige V. *My Pet Mini Horse*. Minneapolis, Minn.: Bellwether Media, 2020.

Silverman, Buffy. *Mini Pigs*. Minneapolis, Minn.: Lerner Publications, 2018.

Wood, Alix. *Mini Pigs*. London, U.K.: Windmill Books, 2017.

## ON THE WEB

**FACTSURFER**

Factsurfer.com gives you a safe, fun way to find more information.

1. Go to www.factsurfer.com.

2. Enter "mini pigs" into the search box and click 🔍.

3. Select your book cover to see a list of related web sites.

# INDEX

The images in this book are reproduced through the courtesy of: Creative Travel Projects, front cover (background); Grigorita Ko, front cover (small pig), 4, 5, 10, 18; JIANG HONGYAN, front cover (hero); Roninnw, pp. 2-3; Juniors/ SuperStock, p. 6; Eriklam, p. 7; LeoniekvanderVliet, p. 8; Tom Klimmeck, p. 9; Mark Kelly/ Alamy, p. 11; RichLegg, p. 11 (inset); Mint Images Limited/ Alamy, p. 12; Anna Vershynina, p. 13 (top), 21; New Africa, p. 13 (middle), 17 (middle); Linn Currie, p. 13 (bottom); Bozidar Acimov, p. 14; schubbel, p. 15; Page Light Studios, p. 16; Anke van Wyk, p. 17 (top left); Alexandr Makarov, p. 17 (top right); gcafotografia, p. 17 (bottom); Janet Horton/ Alamy, p. 19; Mint Images/ SuperSTock, p. 20; cynoclub, p. 23.